THE DELIGHTS *of* CHINESE COOKING

by Rebecca Hsu Hui Min

Translated by Margaret Happel

PRENTICE-HALL, INC.

Englewood Cliffs, N. J.

The Delights of Chinese Cooking
by Rebecca Hsu Hui Min
This translation copyright © 1971 by Margaret Happel
Copyright © 1966 by Albert Müller Verlag, AG, Rüschlikon-Zürich
First American Edition published by Prentice-Hall, Inc., 1971

ISBN 0-13-197848-9
Library of Congress Catalog Card Number: 78-158194
Printed in the United States of America T

Chinese cuisine is one of total harmony, designed to delight the eye as well as the palate. Each dish is distinguished by its own color, texture and symmetry, and is an integral part of the pleasing whole. The actual cooking process, on the other hand, is simplicity itself.

Sound too good to be true? Not at all.

The history of Chinese cookery winds back over 40 centuries, with the happy result that it is today highly refined and simplified. As the Chinese artist creates a painting with a few deft brush strokes, so does the average cook create a lovely meal, delicate but satisfying, with minimum fuss and bother.

The ingredients for a Chinese meal may be prepared for cooking, and arranged attractively on a platter, well in advance of cooking time. No last-minute chopping, weighing and measuring should keep the hostess stranded in the kitchen. These ingredients are frequently chopped into the same relative size and shape, so that the cooking is speedy. Slowest to cook ingredients go first into the electric skillet or chafing dish, to be followed in logical order by those which need less and less time. This can frequently be done at the table, to the admiring gaze of assembled guests.

Expect to find very lean meats in Chinese cookery, and vegetables which are crisp-cooked for the retention of vitamins and minerals. Sauces are used sparingly, to lightly coat, rather than mask food. Emphasis is placed on contrasts of sweet and sour, hot and cool, crunchy and creamy.

Rice—as important to the Orient as bread is to the Occident—is traditionally cooked without salt, in a manner which goes against every Western cooking rule. For each 1½ cups *cold* water, use 1 cup long-grain rice and bring quickly to a boil. Lower flame and simmer rice, covered, for 20 minutes. Cooked rice, incidentally, may be kept in the refrigerator for several days (ideal to have on hand if you want to prepare fried rice).

Vegetable oils, such as soy, peanut and safflower oils, are used in cooking, rather than animal fats. Olive oil is avoided, as its distinctive flavor can be overpowering. Ingredients are added to the oil when it is *piping* hot, to seal in natural juices. Chinese cooks traditionally heat the pan first, adding the oil when the pan is hot, but this can be a messy process.

Three menus have been devised to help with the planning of an authentic Chinese meal. Each menu calls for three or four main-course dishes. Depending on appetites, and on the cook's free time, only one or two main courses could be served. One dish should not be omitted, however, and that is the ubiquitous bowl of rice. Rice is the focal point of the Chinese meal, while the meat, poultry and fish offerings are regarded as mere side dishes.

These menus are designed to guide, rather than rule, so that substitutions may be made at will.

Menu One
Almond Chicken (recipe 1)
Sweet–Sour Pork (12)
Crab Foo Yong (29)
Minced Chicken in Sweet Corn Soup (34)
Almond Tea (44)

Menu Two
Spring Rolls (37)
Beef with Green Peppers (22)
Pork and Vegetables with Vermicelli and Egg Topping (14)
Hot and Sour Soup (36)
Toffee Apples (41)

Menu Three
Fried Fish with Sweet–Sour Sauce (23)
Chicken with Coconut (2)
Pork Fillet with Black Bean Sauce (13)
Vermicelli and Vegetable Soup (35)
Peking Dust (43)

Once you have cooked your Chinese meal, how best to serve it?

There is no set sequence in the serving of a typically Chinese meal. Rice, soup, side dishes and often dessert as well, are placed on the table together. At a Chinese banquet where as many as thirty dishes may be offered, eight dishes might be placed on the table at once and guests will choose from each.

The table should be set with a small bowl of rice at each place, a small plate for side dishes, a soup bowl (and, if possible, a porcelain spoon), a small dish for sauce and another for dessert. In the center of the table, place bowls containing condiments such as soy sauce, mustard, catsup and the like.

Seating arrangements are, naturally, a matter of taste; in China, the host couple sit side by side, facing the guests of honor, who also sit side by side.

As for chopsticks, they should be provided only if their use is a pleasure to all concerned. Struggling with them is unnecessary. Try placing them on the table, along with traditional Western cutlery, and let guests use them as they wish.

This book is intended as a guide to the basics of typical Chinese cuisine. The recipes are simple and authentic, incorporating just the right amount of Chinese tradition. Even the recipes in which boiling water is poured through the chicken have techniques based in pure Chinese logic, for this method insures sealing in of meat juices and an immediate cooking of meat from outside. The ingredients and cooking equipment used are available in virtually every metropolitan area. If you can't find the right ingredient, or don't own the proper cooking pot, make substitutions.

Brief descriptions of popular ingredients follow.

Monosodium glutamate: Many Chinese dishes call for this ingredient, which serves to accentuate the specific aroma and flavor of the meat or vegetable with which it is used. However, this is an optional extra.

Bamboo shoots: These may be purchased canned and are halved and salted, or whole and unsalted. We prefer them whole and unsalted, but if you can't find them, use the salted variety, remembering to adjust the salt in the recipe accordingly.

Ginger: The fresh root is available in some metropolitan areas. Ginger in jars, preserved in juice, is also frequently available and may be used if rinsed first. Several recipes that follow call for ginger juice. Squeeze ginger root in a garlic press to extract juice.

Dried Chinese mushrooms: Soak in warm water at least 30 minutes before using. These are to be found in some supermarkets and delicatessens. If you can't find them, use regular fresh mushrooms.

Bean curd: Produced from soy beans, this ingredient has no substitute. However, it is never essential to any of these recipes—just a tasty addition.

Vermicelli: These noodles, made from rice or tapioca, are cut into the length desired, washed and soaked one hour before using.

Cornstarch: Dredge meat and fish in it; use it in marinades and as a thickening for soups and gravies. It is lighter than flour, and is used constantly in Chinese cuisine.

Oyster sauce: This is called for several times in the recipes that follow. Bottles of oyster sauce are sold in Chinese markets, but why not make your own? Whir 2 (8-oz.) cans oysters and liquid in blender until completely liquidized. Simmer, covered, 20 minutes, then strain. Stir in 2 tablespoons soy sauce and bottle. *Store in refrigerator.* Will keep about two weeks.

Sesame paste: Buy in Oriental stores or grind sesame seeds in blender to form paste.

To start your Chinese feast in the proper fashion, all that remains is for the hostess to tell her guests in Canton Chinese, "Yum sing" . . . which is to say, "Please help yourself."

1 (2½-pound) whole roasting chicken

Seasoning for Chicken
1 tablespoon *each* dry sherry or Chinese rice wine and soy sauce
2 teaspoons salt
⅛ teaspoon *each* pepper and monosodium glutamate

3 quarts salted water
1 tablespoon oil
1 green pepper, cubed
1 red pepper, cubed

Sauce
1 tablespoon butter
1 tablespoon flour
½ cup chicken broth
¼ cup pineapple juice
⅛ teaspoon *each* salt and pepper
Cubed white meat from half a coconut
2 slices pineapple, cubed
1 apple, peeled and cubed
1 banana, sliced

Method

Wash chicken well and pat dry. Blend together seasoning ingredients and rub thoroughly into chicken, inside and out. Let stand 1 hour.

Bring salted water to a boil in a deep pan. Hold chicken over boiling water. Using a glass measuring cup, pour boiling water *through* chicken five or six times. Cut chicken in quarters and add to boiling water. Cook, covered, 30 minutes. Drain. Cut each quarter in half and place on serving dish.

In a medium skillet, heat oil until very hot. Stir-fry green and red pepper cubes for 5 seconds only. Set aside.

In the same skillet make sauce by melting butter and stirring in flour. Blend in broth, pineapple juice, salt and pepper. Bring to a boil, stirring constantly. Add prepared, cubed coconut and fruit and cook just until fruit is heated through. Add pepper cubes. Pour hot sauce over chicken. Serves 4.

1 (2½-pound) whole roasting chicken

Seasoning for Chicken
2 tablespoons dry sherry or Chinese rice wine
2 teaspoons salt
1 teaspoon monosodium glutamate

3 quarts salted water

Marinade
½ cup *each* brandy or Chinese rice wine and chicken broth
2 teaspoons salt
1 teaspoon monosodium glutamate

Method

Wash chicken well and pat dry. Blend together seasoning ingredients and rub thoroughly into chicken, inside and out. Let stand 1 hour.

Bring salted water to a boil in a deep pan. Hold chicken over boiling water. Using a glass measuring cup, pour boiling water through chicken five or six times.

Truss chicken, tying legs together and skewering wings to body, and add to boiling water. Cook, covered, 45 minutes to 1 hour, until chicken is tender. Drain and place in bowl.

Bring marinade ingredients quickly to a boil. Pour over chicken and refrigerate at least 2 hours. Turn frequently so that chicken absorbs marinade evenly. Drain and serve whole, chilled, as pictured, or divide into quarters. Serves 4.

1 large or 2 small, whole chicken breasts, boned
2 teaspoons cornstarch
⅛ teaspoon *each* salt, pepper and monosodium glutamate

Mushrooms and Bamboo Shoots
6 large black Chinese mushrooms, softened and cut in strips
1 (8-oz.) can bamboo shoots, in julienne strips
¼ cup chicken broth
1½ teaspoons soy sauce
⅛ teaspoon *each* salt, pepper and monosodium glutamate

1 quart oil for deep-frying

Marinade
1 egg white
1 tablespoon *each* soy sauce and dry sherry or Chinese rice wine

Sauce
1 tablespoon oil
2 thin slices ginger root, chopped
1 scallion, cut in ½-inch pieces
1 small clove garlic, chopped
2 tablespoons *each* chicken broth and oyster sauce
1 tablespoon *each* dry sherry or Chinese rice wine, cornstarch, soy sauce and oil
¼ teaspoon *each* salt, pepper, sugar and monosodium glutamate

Method

Remove skin from boned chicken breasts and slice chicken in julienne strips. Toss with cornstarch, salt, pepper and monosodium glutamate. Beat marinade ingredients together and add chicken to marinade, stirring to coat each piece. Cover and set aside.

Toss mushrooms, bamboo shoots, broth, soy sauce and seasonings. Add to 1 tablespoon hot oil in skillet. Simmer 2 minutes, drain and set aside.

Heat 1 quart oil in a large saucepan. Drain chicken from marinade and deep-fry 15 to 30 seconds, until golden. Stir constantly during frying to keep pieces separate. Drain and set aside.

Place 1 tablespoon oil in skillet. Add ginger root, scallion and garlic. Sauté gently until aroma develops. Blend remaining sauce ingredients and add to skillet. Bring to a boil, stirring constantly. Add mushrooms, bamboo shoots and chicken. Heat quickly in sauce, stirring constantly. Serves 2.

1 large or 2 small, whole chicken breasts, boned

Seasoning for Chicken
2 tablespoons dry sherry or Chinese rice wine
2 teaspoons salt
1 teaspoon monosodium glutamate

1 quart oil for deep-frying
2 slices pineapple, cubed
1 small green pepper, cubed
1 small red pepper, cubed

Sauce
1 tablespoon oil
2 thin slices ginger root, chopped
1 scallion, cut in ½-inch pieces
1 small clove garlic, chopped
2 tablespoons *each* tomato catsup and chicken broth
2 teaspoons vinegar
1 teaspoon *each* soy sauce and cornstarch
⅛ teaspoon *each* pepper, sugar and monosodium glutamate

Method

Remove skin from boned chicken breasts and cut chicken into ½-inch cubes. Toss with seasoning ingredients to coat evenly.

Heat 1 quart oil in large saucepan. Add cubed pineapple and peppers. Deep-fry 5 to 10 seconds only. Drain and set aside. Add chicken and deep-fry 15 to 30 seconds, until golden, stirring constantly to keep pieces separate. Drain and set aside.

Place 1 tablespoon oil in skillet. Add ginger root, scallion and garlic and sauté gently until aroma develops. Blend remaining sauce ingredients and add to skillet. Heat, stirring constantly, until thickened. Add pineapple, peppers and chicken. Heat quickly, tossing to coat evenly with sauce. Garnish, as pictured, with additional pineapple. Serves 2.

1 (2½ to 3-pound) whole roasting chicken
1 tablespoon cornstarch
1 teaspoon salt
½ teaspoon *each* sugar and monosodium glutamate
¼ teaspoon powdered cloves

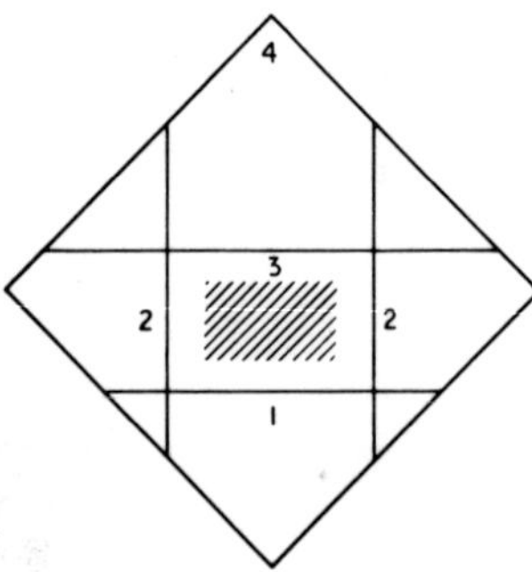

Marinade
1 tablespoon *each* brandy, soy sauce and oil
2 teaspoons ginger juice

1 bunch scallions (about 8 to 10)
Brown paper cut in 4-inch squares
1 quart oil for deep-frying

Method

Skin chicken and cut in quarters. Cut meat from bones in approximately ½x1½-inch strips, each about ¼-inch thick. Toss with cornstarch, salt, sugar, monosodium glutamate and powdered cloves. Toss with marinade ingredients and let stand 1 hour.

Cut scallions in 1½-inch pieces. Place 1 piece each of scallion and chicken in center of a lightly-oiled 4-inch-square of brown paper. Wrap as illustrated in drawing. Tuck corner Number 4 into slot cut in paper.

Heat oil to 400° in deep pan. Add paper packets and immediately remove pan from source of heat and "cook" 5 to 7 minutes. Place pan back over heat and reheat oil with packets to 400°. Drain packets and serve at once. Serves 4.

1 (2½-pound) whole roasting chicken
3 quarts boiling salted water

Seasoning for Chicken
2 tablespoons soy sauce
1 tablespoon dry sherry or Chinese rice wine
1 teaspoon finely chopped ginger root
½ teaspoon salt
¼ teaspoon pepper

Sauce
2 tablespoons oil
6 scallions, cut in ½-inch pieces
1 teaspoon finely chopped ginger root
4 whole peppercorns, crushed
2 anise seeds, crushed
¾ cup soy sauce
1 cup water
2 tablespoons dry sherry or Chinese rice wine
⅛ teaspoon salt

1 teaspoon *each* sugar, monosodium glutamate and cornstarch

Method

Wash chicken well and plunge into deep pan containing boiling salted water. Cook 1 minute; drain well. Blend seasoning ingredients and rub thoroughly into chicken, inside and out. Let stand 1 hour.

Prepare sauce in a large saucepan by heating oil and gently sautéeing scallions, ginger root, peppercorns and anise seed until aroma develops. Add soy sauce and simmer 2 minutes. Hold chicken over saucepan and spoon sauce through chicken 5 or 6 times. Place chicken in sauce over low heat. Cook, turning chicken constantly, until skin becomes deep golden-brown. Add water, 1 tablespoon of the dry sherry or rice wine and salt. Cook, covered, 20 to 30 minutes, until chicken is tender.

Remove chicken from saucepan to serving platter. Blend sugar, monosodium glutamate and cornstarch with remaining sherry or rice wine. Pour into sauce, heat and stir to thicken. Pour sauce over and around chicken. Serves 4.

1 large or 2 small, whole chicken breasts, boned
2 teaspoons cornstarch
1/8 teaspoon *each* salt, pepper and monosodium glutamate

Marinade
1 egg white
1 tablespoon *each* soy sauce and dry sherry or Chinese rice wine

1 quart oil for deep-frying

Sauce
3 small green peppers, diced
1 small red pepper, diced
2 dried black Chinese mushrooms, softened and diced, or 6 small mushrooms, quartered
1/4 cup chicken broth
1 tablespoon soy sauce
1 teaspoon *each* oil and cornstarch
1/8 teaspoon *each* salt, pepper, sugar and monosodium glutamate

Method

Remove skin from boned chicken breasts and cut chicken into 1/2-inch cubes. Toss with cornstarch and seasonings to coat evenly. Beat together marinade ingredients and add chicken to marinade, stirring to coat each piece well.

Heat 1 quart oil in a large saucepan and deep-fry chicken 15 to 30 seconds, until golden. Stir constantly to keep pieces separate. Drain and set aside.

Place 1 tablespoon of the oil in large skillet. Gently sauté green and red peppers and mushrooms until aroma develops. Blend remaining sauce ingredients and add to skillet. Bring to a boil, stirring constantly. Add chicken, tossing with mixture, and reheat quickly. Serves 2.

Egg white

1 egg white
1 tablespoon *each* heavy cream and chicken broth
⅛ teaspoon *each* salt and monosodium glutamate
1 quart oil for deep-frying

1 cup tiny cooked shrimps
6 small mushrooms, quartered
1 tablespoon oil
1 teaspoon dry sherry or Chinese rice wine
⅛ teaspoon *each* salt, pepper and monosodium glutamate

Seasoned Cream

1½ cups heavy cream
1 tablespoon *each* cornstarch and oil
⅛ teaspoon *each* salt and monosodium glutamate

Method

Beat egg white with cream, broth and seasonings. Heat 1 quart oil in deep pan and slowly drizzle egg-white mixture into oil so that it cooks in ribbons. Stir gently to keep ribbons apart, cooking only 15 to 20 seconds. Remove from oil with slotted spoon while white is firm but soft. Set aside.

In a large skillet gently sauté shrimps and mushrooms in 1 tablespoon oil, adding dry sherry or rice wine and seasonings. Cook 2 minutes. Add to skillet 1½ cups heavy cream blended with cornstarch, oil and seasonings. Heat slowly, stirring constantly, until thickened. Add egg white and stir well. Serves 2.

The cooking device in the photograph is a Mongolian hot pot. The broth in the pan is heated by charcoal fire. An ideal Western substitute for this piece of equipment would be a large fondue pot, chafing dish or electric skillet.

1 pound lean lamb shoulder, sliced in thin 1½-inch pieces
½ pound beef fillet, sliced in thin 1½-inch pieces
½ pound lamb kidneys, skinned, cored and quartered
1 pound young spinach leaves
1 small head Romaine lettuce cut in 1½-inch strips
6 dried black Chinese mushrooms, softened and diced, or 18 small mushrooms, quartered

2½ quarts chicken broth

Sauce
1 cup *each* soy sauce and cider vinegar
2 eggs, beaten
½ cup *each* oyster sauce and dry sherry or Chinese rice wine
½ cup *each* chopped parsley, chopped scallions and chopped fennel
Salt, sugar and pepper
½ cup spaghetti, broken in ½-inch pieces

Method

Divide meats evenly between four platters, arranging attractively. Similarly, divide vegetables between the same platters. In center of table place simmering chicken broth. Each person skewers meat and vegetables on chopsticks, metal skewers or fondue forks, and cooks them in the broth. Thirty to sixty seconds is enough time.

Sauce ingredients are placed on the table in separate bowls. Each person mixes sauce to his liking in his own bowl and dips the cooked meat and vegetables in the sauce.

When all the meat is eaten, the remaining vegetables are cooked in the broth with the herbs, eggs and spaghetti to make a delicious soup. The soup is then served as the finale to this memorable and tasty meal. Serves 4.

½ pound pork fillet, sliced in thin 1½-inch pieces
2 teaspoons cornstarch
⅛ teaspoon *each* salt, pepper and monosodium glutamate

Marinade
1 egg white
1 tablespoon *each* soy sauce and dry sherry or Chinese
rice wine

Snow Peas
1 tablespoon oil
¼ pound fresh snow peas or half a (9-oz.) package
frozen snow peas, thawed and dried
½ cup chicken broth
⅛ teaspoon *each* salt and monosodium glutamate

1 quart oil for deep-frying

Sauce
1 tablespoon oil
1 (8-oz.) can bamboo shoots, cut in julienne strips
4 thin slices ginger root, chopped
2 scallions, cut in 1-inch pieces
1 black Chinese mushroom, softened and sliced, or 2
small mushrooms, sliced
2 tablespoons *each* chicken broth and oyster sauce
1 tablespoon dry sherry or Chinese rice wine
1 teaspoon *each* soy sauce and cornstarch
⅛ teaspoon *each* salt, pepper, sugar and monosodium
glutamate

Method

Toss pork strips with cornstarch and seasonings, coating well. Beat together marinade
ingredients and add pork, stirring to coat each piece with marinade.

In a small skillet, heat 1 tablespoon oil quickly and add snow peas, broth and seasonings. Simmer 15 seconds. Drain and set aside.

Heat 1 quart oil in deep pan. Add pork and remove from heat. Cook meat, off heat, 15
seconds, stirring to keep pieces separate. Drain and set aside.

Place 1 tablespoon oil in a large skillet and gently sauté bamboo shoots, ginger root,
scallions and mushrooms, cooking until aroma develops. Blend remaining sauce ingredients and add to skillet. Heat slowly, stirring constantly, until sauce is thickened. Add
snow peas and pork and toss to coat well. Reheat quickly. Serves 2.

1 tablespoon *each* soy sauce and dry sherry or Chinese rice wine
1 egg
⅛ teaspoon *each* salt, pepper and monosodium glutamate
¾ pound lean pork shoulder, cut in ¾-inch cubes
¼ cup cornstarch

1 pint (2 cups) oil for deep-frying

Sauce
2 slices pineapple, each cut in 8 pieces
1 (8-oz.) can bamboo shoots
1 green pepper, cut in ½-inch cubes
1 red pepper, cut in ½-inch cubes

½ cup vinegar
2 tablespoons pineapple juice
2 tablespoons tomato catsup
¼ cup sugar
2 teaspoons cornstarch
1 teaspoon soy sauce
⅛ teaspoon *each* salt and monosodium glutamate

Method

Beat together soy sauce, dry sherry or rice wine, egg and seasonings. Toss with pork cubes to coat well and sprinkle with cornstarch. Toss again to keep pieces separate.

Heat oil in a large skillet. Fry pork cubes, a few at a time, until golden brown. Reheat oil and add cooked pork all at once, to crisp and brown thoroughly. Drain and place on serving platter. Keep hot.

Pour off oil from skillet, reserving 1 tablespoon. Add pineapple, bamboo shoots and peppers. Gently sauté until aroma develops.

In a small bowl, blend remaining ingredients and stir into skillet. Heat slowly, stirring, until sauce thickens. Pour over hot pork. Serves 4.

½ pound pork fillet or shoulder, cut in ¾-inch cubes
2 teaspoons cornstarch
⅛ teaspoon *each* salt, pepper and monosodium glutamate

Marinade
1 egg white
1 tablespoon *each* soy sauce and dry sherry or Chinese rice wine

1 quart oil for deep-frying

Sauce
1 tablespoon oil
6 thin slices ginger root, chopped
3 cloves garlic, slivered
2 tablespoons canned black beans, finely chopped
1 leek or scallion, cut in 1½-inch pieces
½ of a green or red pepper, diced
¼ cup chicken broth
1 tablespoon soy sauce
⅛ teaspoon *each* salt, sugar and monosodium glutamate

1 teaspoon cornstarch

Method

Toss pork cubes with cornstarch and seasonings to coat well. Beat together marinade ingredients and add pork, tossing to coat evenly.

Heat 1 quart oil in a deep saucepan. Deep-fry pork 30 to 40 seconds, until light brown. Drain and set aside, keeping hot.

In a large skillet in 1 tablespoon oil, gently sauté ginger, garlic, black beans, scallion and diced pepper until aroma develops. Add all ingredients *except* cornstarch. Simmer, covered, 2 minutes. Stir in cornstarch, blended with a little water. Bring quickly to a boil, stirring constantly, and pour over hot pork. Serves 2.

¼ pound pork fillet or pork shoulder, cut in thin strips
2 teaspoons cornstarch
⅛ teaspoon *each* pepper and monosodium glutamate
1 tablespoon *each* soy sauce and dry sherry or Chinese rice wine
1 tablespoon oil
1 scallion, cut in thin strips

Vegetables
1 tablespoon oil
1 (8-oz.) can bamboo shoots, cut in thin strips
½ cup thinly sliced preserved bean curd (optional)
10 black Chinese mushrooms, softened and cut in thin strips, or 4 tiny mushrooms, cut in thin strips
¼ cup transparent Chinese noodles or vermicelli (break into ½-inch pieces)

1 tablespoon *each* dry sherry or Chinese rice wine and soy sauce

½ cup *each* thinly sliced celery and canned bean sprouts, drained

Sauce
2 tablespoons chicken broth
1 tablespoon dry sherry or Chinese rice wine
1 teaspoon *each* soy sauce and oil
½ teaspoon cornstarch
⅛ teaspoon *each* salt and monosodium glutamate

Egg Topping
2 eggs
1 tablespoon water
1 teaspoon oil

Method

Toss thinly sliced pork with cornstarch and seasonings, coating well. Sprinkle with soy sauce and sherry or rice wine and let stand 15 minutes. Heat oil in skillet and stir-fry pork and scallion 30 seconds. Remove and set aside.

In the same skillet, heat 1 tablespoon oil and add all vegetable ingredients. Toss well. Simmer, covered, over very low heat for 5 minutes. Add celery, bean sprouts and reserved pork and scallion. Toss well.

In a small bowl, blend sauce ingredients and add to skillet. Cook to thicken sauce and coat vegetables and meat. Place on serving platter and keep hot.

Whisk eggs and water together. Heat 1 teaspoon oil in skillet and sauté eggs until golden on one side. Do not fold or turn. Place on top of meat and vegetables, as pictured. Serves 2.

2 to 2½ pounds pork shoulder or butt, with bone in
6 slices ginger root
2 scallions, cut in 1-inch pieces
¼ cup soy sauce

1 quart oil for deep-frying

Sauce
½ cup *each* soy sauce and dry sherry or Chinese rice wine
2 tablespoons *each* sugar and finely chopped ginger root
2 scallions, cut in ½-inch pieces
½ teaspoon monosodium glutamate
⅛ teaspoon *each* salt and crushed anise seeds

3 heads Bibb lettuce or 2 heads Boston lettuce

Method

Place pork in a large pan and cover with water. Add ginger root and scallions and simmer, covered, for 1½ hours, or until pork is just tender. Remove from pan and cool slightly. Rub all over with soy sauce.

Heat 1 quart oil in deep pan and add pork. Fry, covered, turning from time to time, until meat is crisp and golden-brown. Place on platter and keep warm.

Combine sauce ingredients in medium pan. Simmer, covered, until reduced by half. Add Bibb lettuce heads, halved (if using Boston lettuce, quarter each head). Cover and cook 15 seconds, to heat lettuce. Shake pan constantly. Arrange lettuce around pork, as pictured, and pour sauce over meat. Serves 4.

2 pounds lean pork shoulder in one piece, bone re-
moved

Marinade
⅓ cup sugar
2 tablespoons salt
¼ teaspoon monosodium glutamate
1 shallot or scallion, finely chopped
1 clove garlic, finely chopped
3 tablespoons brandy
1 tablespoon soy sauce
1 teaspoon ginger juice

2 teaspoons honey

Sauce
½ cup *each* soy bean paste, oyster sauce and sesame
paste
2 tablespoons *each* sugar and water
1 tablespoon *each* oil and brandy

1 tablespoon oil
2 cloves garlic, finely chopped
1 shallot or scallion, finely chopped

Method

Cut pork into 1-inch strips measuring 9 inches in length by 2 inches wide. Combine marinade ingredients and rub into all meat surfaces. Let stand 1 hour. Broil or barbecue 4 inches from source of heat for 25 minutes, turning twice. Brush with honey 5 minutes before end of cooking time.

Meanwhile, make sauce by combining all sauce ingredients except oil, garlic and shallot or scallion. Let stand. In a small skillet, heat oil and gently sauté garlic and shallot or scallion. Add to sauce.

Cut hot meat in thin slices and dip each piece into hot sauce before eating. Serves 4.

1½ pounds ground lean pork
4 thin slices ginger root, finely chopped
2 scallions, finely chopped

Seasonings for Pork
1 egg
1 tablespoon *each* soy sauce and dry sherry or Chinese rice wine
½ teaspoon *each* salt and cornstarch

2 cups chicken broth
4 slices ginger root
2 scallions, cut in 1-inch pieces

Sauce
2 tablespoons oil
2 scallions, cut in ½-inch pieces
2 thin slices ginger root, finely chopped
¼ cup *each* soy sauce and dry sherry or Chinese rice wine
1 teaspoon *each* sugar and cornstarch
½ teaspoon monosodium glutamate
⅛ teaspoon salt and pepper

Vegetable
1 pound young spinach leaves or 1 pound Chinese cabbage, cut in 3-inch pieces
2 tablespoons oil
⅛ teaspoon *each* salt and monosodium glutamate

Method

Mix thoroughly ground pork, ginger root, scallions and pork seasonings. Divide mixture into four equal balls. In a deep pan, boil chicken broth with ginger root and scallions. Add meat balls to broth, one at a time, without interrupting the boiling. Simmer, uncovered, 20 minutes. Drain.

In a large skillet, prepare sauce by heating oil and browning scallions and ginger root. Blend remaining sauce ingredients in a small bowl and add to skillet. Heat, stirring constantly, until sauce is thickened. Add meat balls and heat, turning constantly to glaze meat. Cook about 5 to 7 minutes. Place on serving platter and pour any remaining sauce over meat. Keep hot.

Prepare vegetables by tossing pieces of spinach or cabbage in skillet with 2 tablespoons hot oil. Add seasonings. Stir-fry 2 to 3 minutes and place around meat balls. Serves 4.

¼ pound lean veal, sliced in thin 2-inch strips
2 teaspoons cornstarch
⅛ teaspoon *each* salt, pepper and monosodium glutamate
1 egg white
1 tablespoon dry sherry or Chinese rice wine
1 teaspoon soy sauce

Cauliflower
¼ head cauliflower, in sprigs
1 tablespoon oil
¼ cup chicken broth
⅛ teaspoon *each* salt, pepper and monosodium glutamate

Snow Peas
¼ pound fresh snow peas or ½ (9-oz.) package frozen snow peas, thawed and dried

1 teaspoon oil
¼ cup chicken broth
⅛ teaspoon *each* salt, pepper and monosodium glutamate

2 cups oil

Sauce
1 tablespoon oil
4 mushrooms, thinly sliced
2 thin slices ginger root, finely chopped
1 scallion, cut in ½-inch pieces
1 small garlic clove, finely chopped

2 tablespoons chicken broth
1 tablespoon soy sauce
½ teaspoon cornstarch
⅛ teaspoon *each* salt, pepper, sugar and monosodium glutamate

Method

Toss veal strips with cornstarch and seasonings to coat well. Beat together egg white, sherry or rice wine and soy sauce and toss with veal, coating each piece. Set aside.

In a small skillet, toss cauliflower sprigs in 1 tablespoon hot oil. Add broth and seasonings and simmer 2 minutes. Drain and set aside. In same skillet, toss snow peas in 1 teaspoon hot oil. Add broth and seasonings and simmer 15 seconds. Drain and set aside.

Heat 2 cups oil. Add veal and remove from heat. While oil is off the heat, deep-fry veal, stirring constantly, for 2 minutes. Drain and set aside.

In a large skillet, heat 1 tablespoon oil. Gently sauté mushrooms, ginger root, scallion and garlic until aroma develops. Blend together remaining ingredients and add to pan. Heat, stirring constantly, until thickened. Add veal and vegetables. Cook only to heat through. Serves 2.

1 pound lean beef (fillet or sirloin), thinly sliced
1 tablespoon cornstarch
¼ teaspoon *each* baking powder and monosodium glutamate
⅛ teaspoon salt

½ cup water
1 teaspoon *each* soy sauce and dry sherry or Chinese rice wine

2 tablespoons oil

1 quart oil for deep-frying

Sauce
1 tablespoon oil
3 thin slices ginger, finely chopped
1 scallion, cut in ½-inch strips
1 small clove garlic, finely chopped

2 tablespoons *each* chicken broth and oyster sauce
1 tablespoon *each* dry sherry or Chinese rice wine and soy sauce
1 teaspoon cornstarch

4 dried black Chinese mushrooms, softened and thinly sliced

Method

Rub beef strips well with cornstarch and seasonings. Add water, seasoned with soy sauce and sherry or rice wine, and gently press meat in liquid so that liquid is absorbed. Add oil and again press meat to absorb oil. Let stand 1 hour.

In a deep pan, heat 1 quart oil. Deep-fry meat strips for 15 to 20 seconds, until color changes. Drain and set aside.

In a large skillet, heat 1 tablespoon oil. Gently sauté ginger, scallion and garlic until aroma develops. Blend remaining sauce ingredients in a small bowl and add to skillet with ginger mixture. Heat and stir to thicken. Add beef and mushrooms to skillet and stir thoroughly, cooking only to reheat. Serves 2.

1 pound lean beef (fillet or sirloin), thinly sliced
1 tablespoon cornstarch
1 teaspoon monosodium glutamate
½ teaspoon salt
¼ teaspoon baking powder

½ cup water
1 tablespoon *each* soy sauce and dry sherry or Chinese rice wine
1 teaspoon ginger juice
2 tablespoons oil

3 tablespoons oil for deep-frying
1 thin slice ginger root, finely chopped
1 small clove garlic, finely chopped

Sauce
2 tablespoons *each* tomato catsup, dry sherry or Chinese rice wine and water
1 tablespoon oil
1 teaspoon *each* Worcestershire sauce and cornstarch
¼ teaspoon *each* salt and sugar

Method

Rub beef strips very well with cornstarch and seasonings. Add water, seasoned with soy sauce and sherry or rice wine and ginger juice, and gently press meat so that water is absorbed. Add 2 tablespoons oil and again press meat to absorb oil. Let stand 1 hour.

Heat 3 tablespoons oil in skillet and add ginger, garlic and meat. Fry over high heat for 15 to 20 seconds. Remove from skillet. Blend all sauce ingredients in the same skillet. Heat and stir until thickened and add beef, cooking only to reheat. Garnish as pictured. Serves 2.

Marinade

2 tablespoons soy sauce
1 tablespoon brandy
1 teaspoon salt
¼ teaspoon pepper
2½ pounds beef sirloin, cut in ¾-inch cubes

1 quart oil for deep-frying
¼ cup flour

Sauce

1 tablespoon oil
8 scallions, cut in 1½-inch pieces
4 thin slices ginger root, finely chopped
3 cloves garlic, crushed
3 anise seeds, crushed
10 peppercorns
½ cup soy sauce
2 tablespoons brandy

½ cup chicken broth

2 tablespoons water
1 teaspoon *each* cornstarch and sugar

1 teaspoon oil

Method

Beat together marinade ingredients and add beef cubes, stirring to coat each piece thoroughly.

Heat 1 quart oil in large saucepan. Drain beef from marinade and toss with flour to coat evenly. Brown beef cubes, a few at a time, about 1 minute in oil. Drain and set aside.

Place 1 tablespoon oil in skillet. Add all sauce ingredients *except* broth and sauté gently while mixing. Add broth to skillet slowly, then add beef and simmer, covered, for 2 hours.

Blend water, cornstarch and sugar and stir into beef mixture. Heat until thickened, stirring constantly. Stir in oil. Garnish with a few pieces of chopped scallion. Serve at once. Serves 4.

2 pounds lean beef (fillet or sirloin), thinly sliced
1 tablespoon cornstarch
¼ teaspoon *each* baking powder, monosodium glutamate and salt

½ cup water
1 teaspoon soy sauce
½ teaspoon *each* dry sherry or Chinese rice wine and ginger juice

2 tablespoons oil

Sauce
1 tablespoon cold water
1 teaspoon cornstarch

1 tablespoon oyster sauce
½ teaspoon *each* soy sauce and stock
¼ teaspoon *each* salt, sugar, monosodium glutamate and oil

1 quart oil for deep-frying

2 tablespoons oil
1 green pepper, cut in ¼-inch strips
¼ cup sliced mushrooms
3 thin slices ginger root
3 scallions, cut in 1½-inch strips
½ garlic clove, minced

1 teaspoon dry sherry or Chinese rice wine

Method

Rub beef strips thoroughly with cornstarch and seasonings. Add water, seasoned with soy sauce, sherry or rice wine and ginger juice. Gently press meat so that liquid mixture is absorbed. Add oil and again press meat so that oil is absorbed. Let stand 1 hour.

Blend cold water and cornstarch and add sauce ingredients. Mix thoroughly and let stand 1 hour.

Drain marinade from beef and deep-fry in 1 quart hot oil for 15 seconds, stirring constantly to keep pieces separated. Remove meat and drain.

Heat 2 tablespoons oil in skillet and add pepper strips. Sauté for 15 seconds, then add mushrooms, ginger root, scallions and garlic. Stir. Add sauce ingredients. Bring to a boil. Then add meat and heat 1 minute. Remove from heat and sprinkle with sherry or rice wine, stirring lightly. Serves 3 to 4.

1 pound fish fillets (whitefish, flounder, sole)

Marinade
2 tablespoons soy sauce
¼ teaspoon powdered thyme
⅛ teaspoon pepper
flour

Batter
3 tablespoons flour
1 tablespoon cornstarch
½ teaspoon baking powder
¼ teaspoon powdered thyme
1 egg
1 tablespoon *each* oil and water

1 quart oil

Sauce
1 tablespoon oil
3 tablespoons *each* cider vinegar and sugar
1 tablespoon tomato catsup
1 clove garlic, crushed
1 teaspoon soy sauce
¾ teaspoon monosodium glutamate
⅛ teaspoon salt
2 teaspoons cornstarch
½ cup chicken broth
1 (8-oz.) can fruit cocktail, drained

Method

Cut fish fillets into 2-inch strips. Rub well with marinade ingredients. Dredge each piece with flour. Shake to remove surplus. Let fish stand 30 minutes.

Blend all batter ingredients together, stirring until smooth. Add fish to batter. Toss gently to coat each piece. Heat 1 quart oil in large saucepan. Fry fish, a few pieces at a time, until golden brown. Drain fish from oil. Place on serving platter. Keep warm.

Place 1 tablespoon oil in skillet. Add all sauce ingredients, except fruit, blending cornstarch with chicken broth before adding. Cook slowly, stirring constantly until thickened. Add fruit cocktail. Heat and pour over fish. Serves 2.

A whole fish, weighing 1 to 1½ pounds

Marinade
1 tablespoon *each* soy sauce, and dry sherry or Chinese rice wine
¼ teaspoon *each* monosodium glutamate, salt and pepper

¼ pound pork cutlet
1 teaspoon *each* soy sauce, dry sherry or Chinese rice wine and flour

Sauce
2 tablespoons *each* dry sherry or Chinese rice wine, soy sauce and chicken broth
1 teaspoon sugar
¼ teaspoon *each* monosodium glutamate and salt

¼ cup oil
3 scallions, cut in 1½-inch pieces
3 thin slices ginger root

¼ cup bamboo shoots, thinly sliced
6 dried black Chinese mushrooms, softened, or 18 small mushrooms, thinly sliced

Method

Carefully clean fish and pat dry. Make 4 diagonal cuts (no deeper than ½-inch) on back of fish to allow marinade to penetrate. Mix marinade ingredients and rub into fish. Let stand 30 minutes.

Cut pork cutlet into thin slices and turn slices to coat in a mixture of soy sauce and dry sherry or rice wine. Sprinkle with flour. Blend all sauce ingredients.

Heat oil in skillet and add scallions and ginger root, sautéeing until slightly browned. Remove from skillet and discard. Place fish in skillet and sauté gently until slightly browned. Add bamboo shoots, mushrooms, pork and sauce to fish. Cover and bring to a boil. Simmer 15 minutes. Serves 2.

A whole fish, weighing 2½ to 3 pounds

Marinade
2 tablespoons soy sauce
1 tablespoon rosé wine or brandy
¼ teaspoon monosodium glutamate

3 thin slices ginger root
6 scallions, cut in 1½-inch pieces
10 small mushrooms, sliced
1 thin slice boiled ham, cut into 8 squares
6 slices bamboo shoot

Sauce
2 tablespoons oil
1 cup cold chicken broth
1 tablespoon cornstarch
1 teaspoon soy sauce

Method

Carefully clean fish, then pat dry. Mix marinade ingredients, rub into fish and let stand for 30 minutes.

Place half the above amount of ginger root, scallions and mushrooms in a colander or sieve. On top of this, place fish, then top with ham, bamboo shoots and remainder of the ginger root, scallions and mushrooms.

Bring enough water to boil in a large saucepan to steam fish without touching colander. Place colander in saucepan, cover and steam fish for 20 minutes.

In a small saucepan, heat oil. Mix broth with cornstarch and add soy sauce. Blend well while heating to thicken. Serve with fish. Serves 4.

1½ pounds shelled, cooked shrimps
1 egg white, slightly beaten
½ teaspoon cornstarch
¼ teaspoon salt
2 cups oil for deep-frying

Sauce
½ teaspoon cornstarch
1 teaspoon cold water
2 teaspoons chicken broth
1 teaspoon *each* dry sherry or Chinese rice wine and soy sauce
¼ teaspoon *each* monosodium glutamate, salt and pepper

2 tablespoons oil
1 cup cooked green peas
2 teaspoons dry sherry or Chinese rice wine

Method

Toss shelled, cooked shrimps with mixture of slightly beaten egg white, cornstarch and salt. Deep-fry in hot oil for 15 seconds, then remove and drain on absorbent paper.

Mix cornstarch with cold water and add to broth and seasonings.

Heat 2 tablespoons oil in a large skillet. Add fried shrimps, cooked green peas and dry sherry or rice wine. Add sauce and stir constantly over high heat until thoroughly mixed and heated. Serves 4.

1½ pounds shelled, cooked large shrimps

Marinade
2 tablespoons soy sauce
¼ teaspoon monosodium glutamate
⅛ teaspoon pepper
1 tablespoon flour

Batter
¼ cup flour
2 tablespoons cornstarch
1 teaspoon baking powder
1 tablespoon melted shortening *or* oil
2 eggs, slightly beaten
2 tablespoons water
¼ teaspoon *each* monosodium glutamate, salt and pepper

1 quart oil for deep-frying

Sauce
1 tablespoon oil
½ cup chicken broth
3 tablespoons sugar
2 tablespoons vinegar
1 tablespoon tomato catsup
1 teaspoon soy sauce
½ teaspoon monosodium glutamate
½ garlic clove, minced
¼ teaspoon salt

1 tablespoon cold water
2 teaspoons cornstarch

Method

Rub shrimps with marinade ingredients and coat with flour. Let stand.

To prepare batter, sift together flour, cornstarch and baking powder. Add remaining batter ingredients and blend thoroughly. Turn shrimps into batter and coat each one well.

Heat 1 quart oil to 375°F. Add batter-coated shrimps and remove pan from heat at once. Let stand 5 minutes, then return to heat and fry until golden brown. Remove shrimps and drain on absorbent paper.

Heat 1 tablespoon oil in a small saucepan. Add sauce ingredients, blending as they come to a boil. Mix water and cornstarch and add to sauce. Heat until slightly thickened. Pour sauce over fried shrimps and garnish with parsley, if desired. Serves 4.

1 pound tiny, cooked, shelled shrimps
1 egg white, slightly beaten

1 tablespoon cornstarch
¼ teaspoon *each* monosodium glutamate and pepper

1 pint oil

Sauce
1 tablespoon oil
3 scallions, cut in 1½-inch pieces
2 thin slices ginger root
1 clove garlic, crushed

¼ cup chicken broth
2 tablespoons sugar
1 tablespoon tomato paste
1 teaspoon dry sherry or Chinese rice wine
½ teaspoon *each* soy sauce and lemon juice

Method

Toss shrimps in egg white to coat each well. Combine cornstarch, monosodium glutamate and pepper. Sprinkle over shrimps. Toss to coat thoroughly.

Heat 1 pint oil in saucepan until very hot. Add shrimps. Fry 20 seconds, only to crisp coating. Drain shrimps from oil with slotted spoon. Set aside.

Heat 1 tablespoon oil in skillet. Add scallions, ginger and garlic, sautéeing until tender. Add remaining sauce ingredients. Blend and heat. Add shrimps, cooking over high **heat** until very hot. Serve immediately. Serves 4

Crabmeat Mixture
1 (7½-oz.) can crabmeat, drained
10 small mushrooms, diced
¼ cup diced bamboo shoots
¼ teaspoon *each* monosodium glutamate, salt and
pepper

2 egg whites
2 teaspoons chicken broth

5 tablespoons oil

2 teaspoons cold water
1 teaspoon cornstarch
1 small slice cooked ham, finely chopped

Method

Blend all ingredients for crabmeat mixture. Set aside. Beat egg whites with chicken broth until foamy. Heat 4 tablespoons of the oil in skillet and egg-broth mixture. Fry over low heat until smooth but still very soft. Drain from oil.

Add remaining 1 tablespoon oil to skillet and add crabmeat mixture. Mix very quickly and heat for 30 seconds. Stir in cooked egg white-broth mixture. Mix cornstarch and water and add to skillet, cooking until slightly thickened. Sprinkle with finely chopped ham. Serves 2.

1 pound *each* fresh cauliflower and broccoli

Cauliflower
1 tablespoon oil
1 cup chicken broth
¼ teaspoon *each* monosodium glutamate and salt

Broccoli
1 tablespoon *each* oil, broth and dry sherry or Chinese rice wine
½ teaspoon ginger juice
¼ teaspoon *each* soy sauce and sugar
⅛ teaspoon *each* monosodium glutamate and salt

Sauce
1 tablespoon oil
½ cup chicken broth
2 teaspoons cream
¼ teaspoon monosodium glutamate
⅛ teaspoon salt

1 tablespoon cold water
2 teaspoons cornstarch

Method

Prepare cauliflower and broccoli by washing well and removing flowerettes from all stalks.

Heat 1 tablespoon oil in skillet, add cauliflower and ingredients, cooking for 3 minutes.

Mix broccoli ingredients and heat 1 tablespoon oil in a small saucepan. Add broccoli and ingredients and stir-fry for 30 seconds.

Heat 1 tablespoon oil in a small saucepan and add sauce ingredients, cooking for 15 seconds. Mix water and cornstarch and add to sauce, cooking until slightly thickened.

Place cauliflower in the center of a warmed platter and arrange broccoli around it. Pour hot sauce over cauliflower. Serves 4.

½ pound small shrimps
1 tablespoon oil
¼ cup chicken broth
⅛ teaspoon *each* monosodium glutamate, salt and pepper

3 tablespoons peanut oil
20 dried black Chinese mushrooms, softened
½ cup chicken broth
2 tablespoons soy sauce
½ teaspoon sugar
⅛ teaspoon *each* monosodium glutamate and salt

Salad Dressing
2 tablespoons *each* oil and vinegar
1 teaspoon sesame seeds, crushed
½ teaspoon dry mustard
¼ teaspoon *each* monosodium glutamate, salt and pepper

Vegetables
¼ pound cabbage, shredded
Half an 8-oz. can bamboo shoots, shredded
¼ cup *each* bean sprouts and shredded carrot

Method

Shell and devein shrimp. Heat 1 tablespoon oil in a small saucepan and add shrimp, broth and seasonings. Cook for 2 minutes, then cool.

Heat peanut oil. Add mushrooms and cook 2 minutes, then add broth, soy sauce and sugar. Cover and simmer for 25 minutes. Stir in seasonings and let cool. When cooled, slice each mushroom in half.

Mix thoroughly the salad dressing ingredients.

Cook vegetables in lightly salted water just enough to soften slightly, then toss with salad dressing and chill.

To serve, arrange vegetables on platter with shrimp and top with mushrooms. Serves 4.

1 tablespoon oil
½ cup chicken broth
½ teaspoon ginger juice
⅛ teaspoon *each* monosodium glutamate and salt

1 pound small mushrooms, sliced

½ teaspoon dry sherry or Chinese rice wine

Sauce
¼ cup cold chicken broth
2 teaspoons cornstarch
1 tablespoon oyster sauce
1 teaspoon *each* soy sauce and dry sherry or Chinese rice wine

1 tablespoon oil

Method

Heat 1 tablespoon oil in a saucepan and add broth, ginger juice and seasonings. Bring to a boil and add mushrooms, simmering for 10 minutes. Add sherry or rice wine and cook 15 seconds more, then drain mushrooms and set them aside.

To make sauce, mix broth and cornstarch, then add remaining sauce ingredients.

Heat remaining oil in saucepan and add mushrooms and sauce. Toss to coat mushrooms thoroughly. Serves 4.

This exotic soup takes time, effort and an impressive list of ingredients, but truly is well worth the trouble. Shark fin is dried and available *only* in Chinese markets.

Broth
1½ pounds lean pork, cubed
1½ pounds pork bone, cut in small pieces
½ pound ham
1 ham bone
1 small stewing chicken, cut in serving pieces
3 quarts water
4 scallions
1 slice ginger root

1 teaspoon *each* monosodium glutamate and salt

¼ pound shark fins
1 quart water

Method

Marinade
1 teaspoon dry sherry or Chinese rice wine
½ teaspoon cornstarch
1 egg white
¼ teaspoon *each* monosodium glutamate, salt and pepper

¼ pound uncooked breast of chicken, cut in strips
1 cup water

1 tablespoon oil
4 scallions, cut in 1½-inch pieces
1 clove garlic, minced

6 cups clear chicken broth

2 tablespoons dry sherry or Chinese rice wine
1 tablespoon chicken fat
¼ teaspoon salt

¼ cup cold water
1½ tablespoons cornstarch

Place first eight ingredients for broth in a large soup kettle. Bring to a boil, skim off foam, then simmer for 6 hours.

Strain broth through cheesecloth, pressing to extract all liquid from meat. Dispose of meat, and season broth with monosodium glutamate and salt. Set aside.

Simmer shark fins for 2 hours in 1 quart water. Remove fins and set aside, discarding water.

Blend first four marinade ingredients and toss with chicken strips to coat each piece well. Cook in boiling water for 15 seconds, drain and set aside.

Heat oil in a deep saucepan. Add scallions and garlic and sauté gently until aroma develops. Add 6 cups clear chicken broth and shark fins and cook for 10 minutes. Add reserved meat broth, sherry or rice wine, chicken fat and salt. Bring to a boil.

Blend water and cornstarch and add to soup. Boil until the soup thickens. Add reserved chicken strips and serve. Serves 8.

⅓ pound cooked chicken breast, finely ground

Marinade
2 tablespoons water
1 teaspoon soy sauce
¼ teaspoon *each* monosodium glutamate and salt

2 egg whites, slightly beaten

1 tablespoon oil
4 cups chicken broth
1 (10-oz.) package frozen kernel corn, thawed

¼ cup cold water
2 tablespoons cornstarch

1 thin slice ham, finely chopped

Method

Toss finely ground chicken with blended marinade ingredients. Add egg whites and mix to coat thoroughly. Set aside.

Heat oil in a large saucepan. Add chicken broth and corn and bring to a boil, then simmer for 5 minutes. Combine water and cornstarch, add to broth mixture and heat until thickened. Stir in reserved ground chicken and mix well. Sprinkle ham over the top of each serving of soup. Serves 6.

¼ pound pork cutlet, thinly sliced

Marinade
2 tablespoons soy sauce
2 teaspoons flour
⅛ teaspoon *each* monosodium glutamate, salt and
pepper

1 tablespoon oil
1 quart chicken broth
¼ cup thinly sliced bamboo shoots
¼ pound sliced small mushrooms, drained
¼ cup vermicelli

½ cup shredded fresh spinach
2 thin slices cooked ham, cut in 1-inch squares
1 tablespoon dry sherry or Chinese rice wine
1 tablespoon oil
⅛ teaspoon *each* salt and pepper

Method

Toss pork slices with blended marinade ingredients, coating thoroughly. Heat oil in a large saucepan and sauté pork for 15 seconds. Add broth, bamboo shoots, mushrooms and vermicelli. Boil for 10 minutes.

Rinse spinach well, then tear leaves into small pieces, discarding stems. Add to soup with ham, sherry or rice wine, oil, salt and pepper. Stir well to blend thoroughly. Serves 6.

¼ pound pork cutlet, thinly sliced

Marinade
2 tablespoons soy sauce
2 teaspoons flour
⅛ teaspoon *each* monosodium glutamate, salt and pepper

1 tablespoon oil
1 quart chicken broth
¼ cup thinly sliced bamboo shoots
¼ pound small mushrooms, sliced
¼ cup vermicelli

2 tablespoons vinegar
¼ teaspoon *each* salt and pepper
3 eggs, beaten until foamy

¼ cup cold water
2 tablespoons cornstarch

Method

Toss pork slices with first three blended marinade ingredients, coating each piece thoroughly.

Heat oil in a large saucepan and sauté pork for 15 seconds. Add broth, bamboo shoots, mushrooms and vermicelli and boil for 10 minutes. Stir in vinegar, salt, pepper and eggs, adding eggs last.

Mix water and cornstarch and stir into soup; boil until thickened. Serves 6.

½ pound pork fillet, diced
1 teaspoon flour
⅛ teaspoon *each* monosodium glutamate and salt

Dough
2½ cups sifted flour
1 cup *each* water and oil
1 teaspoon salt

1 quart oil for deep-frying

½ cup water
1 tablespoon cornstarch

Vegetables for Filling
1 tablespoon oil
¼ cup *each* diced bamboo shoots and diced Chinese mushrooms
1 teaspoon soy sauce
1 cup shredded spinach leaves

1 tablespoon oil
1 teaspoon *each* dry sherry or Chinese rice wine and soy sauce

3 tablespoons chicken broth
1 teaspoon cornstarch

Method

Toss diced pork with a mixture of flour, monosodium glutamate and salt and let stand.

Heat oil in a small skillet and add all ingredients for vegetable filling *except* spinach. Sauté for 2 minutes, then add spinach and sauté 1 minute more. Remove from skillet and let stand.

Heat additional oil in skillet and add pork. Sauté 3 minutes, then stir in dry sherry or rice wine and soy sauce. Mix well to blend flavors, then stir in vegetables. Blend chicken broth and cornstarch and stir into skillet, heating until thickened.

Mix first three ingredients for dough. Heat ¼ cup oil in a small skillet. Using walnut-sized pieces of dough, pat each into a flat pancake and fry in hot oil until a thin coating develops. Remove from skillet at once and continue this process until all dough is used.

Place 2 teaspoons of filling on each pancake. Mix water and cornstarch and heat to thicken. Roll up pancakes to enclose filling and seal ends with thickened cornstarch.

Heat remaining oil (3¾ cups) and place rolls in hot oil, frying until golden brown. Drain on absorbent paper. Serves 4 as an entree.

¼ pound fresh spinach, chopped
⅛ teaspoon monosodium glutamate

Marinade
3 scallions, finely chopped
3 thin slices ginger root, finely chopped
1 tablespoon chicken broth
1 tablespoon oil
1 teaspoon dry sherry or Chinese rice wine
⅛ teaspoon *each* monosodium glutamate and salt

1 pound cooked lean pork, diced

Dough
2 cups sifted flour
½ cup cold water
¾ cup warm water

1 teaspoon oil
1 cup boiling water

1 tablespoon oil

½ cup water
½ teaspoon vinegar

Method

Cook spinach in boiling water with monosodium glutamate for 3 minutes. Drain.

Mix marinade ingredients and toss with diced pork and spinach. Chill for 30 minutes.

Knead 1 cup of the sifted flour with cold water. Mix remaining flour with warm water, then blend both doughs thoroughly by kneading together. Cover with a damp cloth and let rest 15 minutes.

Roll dough out to 1/16-inch thickness, then cut out circles measuring 3 inches in diameter. Place 2 teaspoons of the pork-spinach mixture on each circle. Fold each circle in half to form a crescent and pinch edges firmly to seal.

Heat 1 teaspoon oil in a large skillet and arrange crescents in skillet. Add boiling water and boil for 2 minutes. Drain water from skillet. Add 1 tablespoon additional oil to skillet containing dumplings and cook, covered, for 3 minutes.

Remove cover and sprinkle dumplings with a little of the mixture of water and vinegar. Re-cover pan and cook 3 more minutes. Continue this sprinkling process until the underside of each dumpling is golden-brown. Will serve 4 as an entree, or serve singly as hors d'oeuvres.

½ pound pork fillet, cut in thin strips

Marinade
1 teaspoon *each* soy sauce and dry sherry or Chinese rice wine
¼ teaspoon *each* monosodium glutamate, salt and pepper

½ pound thin noodles
½ cup oil

3 scallions, cut in 1½-inch pieces
2 thin slices ginger root
8 ounces sliced bamboo shoots

1 cup shredded spinach leaves
½ cup sliced mushrooms
2 thin slices cooked ham, cut in 1-inch pieces
4 tablespoons chicken broth

1 tablespoon water
¼ teaspoon cornstarch

1 tablespoon oil
2 teaspoons *each* dry sherry or Chinese rice wine and soy sauce
¼ teaspoon *each* monosodium glutamate, salt and pepper

Method

Rub pork slices with blended marinade ingredients and let stand.

Cook noodles in slightly salted boiling water for 2 minutes, then drain and toss with 1 tablespoon of the oil. Heat 3 more tablespoons of oil in a large skillet and add cooked noodles. Fry over low heat until light brown. Remove from skillet.

Heat remaining 3 tablespoons oil in the same skillet and add scallions and ginger. Sauté until aroma develops, then add marinated pork and sauté 3 more minutes. To this add bamboo shoots, spinach, mushrooms and ham and mix thoroughly. Add 2 tablespoons of the chicken broth and bring to a boil.

Mix water and cornstarch and stir into pork mixture, heating until thickened.

Heat 1 tablespoon oil in a medium saucepan and add the reserved fried noodles, the remaining 2 tablespoons chicken broth and the rest of the seasonings. Stir to blend. To serve, place noodles on warmed platter and top with pork and vegetables. Serves 4.

¼ pound pork fillet, cut in ½-inch cubes
2 tablespoons oil
3 eggs, beaten until foamy
¼ teaspoon salt

¼ pound small shrimps, cooked, shelled and deveined
2 tablespoons oil
6 dried black Chinese mushrooms, softened and diced,
or 10 small mushrooms, cubed

½ cup slightly cooked green peas

3 tablespoons oil
2 cups cooked rice, cooled
2 tablespoons dry sherry or Chinese rice wine
1 teaspoon soy sauce
⅛ teaspoon *each* salt and pepper

Method

Add pork to 1 tablespoon hot oil in a medium skillet and fry 2 minutes. Remove from pan and set aside.

Heat additional 1 tablespoon oil in skillet and add eggs, beaten with salt. Cook eggs until firm. Cut cooked eggs into small cubes and remove from skillet.

Fry shrimps in oil over high heat for 15 seconds and add mushrooms, peas and pork. Toss to mix well.

Heat remaining 3 tablespoons oil in a medium skillet and add cooked rice, sautéeing until golden brown. Then add dry sherry or rice wine, soy sauce, salt and pepper and stir. Mix pork and egg mixtures with rice and cook just to heat through. Serves 4.

3 crisp, tart apples
2 teaspoons flour

Batter
3 tablespoons flour
2 teaspoons cornstarch
1 egg, slightly beaten
3 tablespoons water

2 cups oil for deep-frying

Frosting
⅔ cup sugar
⅓ cup water
¼ teaspoon vinegar

1 tablespoon oil

1 tablespoon sesame seeds

Method

Peel and core apples and cut each into 6 sections. Toss sections with flour until well coated.

Blend batter ingredients well and toss apples in batter to coat.

Heat oil and place batter-coated apples in oil, frying until golden brown. Remove and drain on absorbent paper.

In a small saucepan, mix frosting ingredients, sugar, water and vinegar. Boil, stirring constantly until mixture thickens. Add oil and continue cooking until frosting turns golden, and a small amount dropped from the tip of a spoon spins a long thread. When frosting reaches this stage, immediately pour it over apple sections and toss carefully to coat each piece of apple with frosting. Sprinkle with sesame seeds and allow to cool. Serve on a slightly oiled plate.

To make coating extra-crisp, serve with a container of cold water and dip each section briefly into cold water just before eating. Serves 4.

2 tablespoons unflavored gelatine
½ cup cold water

1½ cups water
½ cup sugar

½ cup condensed milk
½ teaspoon almond extract

1 (8-oz.) can mandarin orange sections, drained
1 (8-oz.) can pineapple chunks, drained

Method

Dissolve gelatine in cold water.

In a medium saucepan, mix 1½ cups water with sugar and bring to a boil. Remove from heat and stir in softened gelatine. When gelatine is completely dissolved, add milk and almond extract and stir.

Chill until set, then decorate almond jelly with canned fruit, as pictured. Cut into cubes to serve. Serves 4 to 6.

1 (8-oz.) can chestnut purée (purée marron)
¼ cup sugar
1 cup heavy cream, whipped
1 teaspoon candied fruit

½ cup sugar
1 teaspoon light corn syrup

Method

Blend purée with sugar and pass through a sieve. Fold half the whipped cream into purée. Arrange in a shallow bowl and decorate with dabs of remaining whipped cream and candied fruit.

Liquify ½ cup sugar over low heat, being careful not to let it brown. Add corn syrup and boil until mixture reads 300° on candy thermometer. Remove from heat. Dip a thin-tined fork into sugar mixture and pull quickly out of the sugar, spinning long threads.

Arrange threads over top of whipped cream purée. Serves 2.

1 cup water
¼ cup raw rice
2 cups blanched almonds

10 cups water
2 cups sugar
2 teaspoons butter
½ teaspoon almond extract

Method

Soak rice in cold water for 15 minutes, then drain. Put blanched almonds, rice and 1 cup of the water through the fine blade of a food grinder three times or, instead of grinding, whir mixture in electric blender for 1 minute.

Place almond-rice mixture in a large saucepan and add remaining ingredients. Bring to a boil and boil for 7 minutes. This "tea" is a thick and delicious drink served hot in cups. Makes 3 quarts.

This is the Chinese equivalent of Irish coffee—half beverage and half dessert.